cabernet
sauvignon

DISCOVERING EXPLORING ENJOYING

cabernet sauvignon

DISCOVERING EXPLORING ENJOYING

CHRIS LOSH

RYLAND
PETERS
& SMALL
LONDON NEW YORK

Designer Pamela Daniels
Senior Editor Clare Double
Picture Research Emily Westlake
Production Paul Harding
Art Director Gabriella Le Grazie
Publishing Director Alison Starling

Printed and bound in China

10 9 8 7 6 5 4 3 2 1

First published in the United States in 2004
by Ryland Peters & Small, Inc.
519 Broadway, 5th Floor, New York NY 10012
www.rylandpeters.com

Text © Chris Losh 2004
Design and commissioned photography
© Ryland Peters & Small 2004

Library of Congress Cataloging-in-Publication Data

Losh, Chris.
    Cabernet sauvignon : discovering exploring enjoying / Chris Losh.
        p. cm.
    Includes index.
    ISBN 1-84172-701-6
  1. Cabernet (Wine) 2. Wine and wine making. I. Title.
TP548 .L68 2004
641.2'223--dc22
                                    2003027644

contents

Cabernet Sauvignon is the most-planted quality red grape variety in the world. You'll find it everywhere from its French heartland to the foothills of the Andes. For millions of people the world over, Cabernet Sauvignon **is** good red wine—as simple as that. But why has it become so popular?

Well, try saying its name slowly, rolling it around your mouth as though it were the wine itself, and you'll get some clue to its character. Exotic yet understandable, presence with poetry, aristocratic yet familiar. It's a mix as beguiling as that of the wine itself. In fact, given Cabernet's silky charm, deep color, and ability to age for years, the miracle is not so much that it is the world's favorite red grape, but that any others get a look-in. In this book we'll look at where this most regal of grapes has come from, where it's going, and what makes it so special. So sit back, pull a cork—and enjoy!

DISCOVERING

There's one very good reason why the world has fallen in love with Cabernet Sauvignon, and that is the way it so effortlessly mixes romance with reliability.

On one hand, it is the grape behind many of the world's most expensive and prestigious wines; on the other, it's still quite capable of knocking out, for next to nothing, eminently gluggable bottles that are perfect for your Tuesday night pasta. Not all grapes are as at home on the president's table as they are in your kitchen. Cabernet may be a proud, blue-blooded grape, but it is still laudably democratic.

And tolerant, too. Winemakers the world over love it because they can raise the yields in the vineyard, irrigate the bejasus out of it, and generally abuse its good trust. But still it will give them something approaching decent wine at the end of it; wine, moreover, that tastes unmistakably of Cabernet.

Surprisingly, given its aristocratic bearing, Cabernet is not one of the world's oldest grape varieties. It first appeared in Bordeaux in the 17th century, centuries later than its French buddy Merlot. Modern genetic fingerprinting techniques suggest that it came about as the result of a spontaneous pollination between two different varieties that were already grown in the region, Cabernet Franc and Sauvignon Blanc.

So if the scientists have it right, the red king of the 21st century is the lovechild of a middleweight red and a fragrant white. It's not turned out badly, considering.

In the vineyard, Cabernet likes to be given time. It's one of the latest ripening of all grape varieties, usually picked at the tail end of summer and into the start of autumn, which means that it can be susceptible to rain.

flavor

But picking early, before the weather breaks, carries risks, too. Cabernet needs a fair bit of sun to ripen—one of the reasons it has done so well in New World countries. Pick before it's fully ripe, and you get thin, stingy fruit and tannins that could strip the enamel from your teeth. In many respects, Cabernet Sauvignon is the picture of tolerance, but growing it somewhere cool and picking it less than fully ripe isn't an option.

A Cabernet vine, you see, gives small, thick-skinned grapes. Since it is grape skins that are responsible for both color and tannin in a wine, and Cabernet has a high skin-to-pulp ratio, that means plenty of color and plenty of tannin.

Now this is fine, provided it's allied to nice ripe fruit flavors, but if the grapes are picked before those fruit flavors have had a chance to develop, you're going to be left with not much taste, but plenty of mouth-puckering tannin. Not a good thing.

It's one of the reasons that wine buffs get so hung up about vintages, particularly in a place like Bordeaux, which is cooler and less reliable in its weather than most of the New World. Was it warm enough to get the grapes properly ripe? Did it rain around harvest, diluting the taste? These are important factors in assessing how the wine is likely to taste.

The grape has blackcurrant aromas, but also takes in plums, black cherries, and damsons.

So what flavors can you typically expect from your average bottle of Cabernet Sauvignon? Well, the grape is most frequently associated with aromas of blackcurrants or cassis, but its flavor palette also takes in other fruits like plums, black cherries, and damsons, plus non-fruit-related characteristics, such as cedar or tobacco, dark chocolate, mint, and eucalyptus. Since just about all Cabernet Sauvignon spends at least some time aging in oak barrels, you're also likely to find aromas of the wood in there, too—usually vanilla or coconut. However, the flavors don't just depend on the weather that year or goings-on in the cellar, but also on a place's terroir.

"Terroir" is an untranslatable French expression which means, more or less, geography, climate, and soil, but actually somehow stands for more than all of them. It's perhaps best captured (not very poetically) as "the natural characteristics that give a wine its character," and it can vary not just from country to country or region to region, but even vineyard to vineyard.

For Cabernet Sauvignon, these variations are most marked in Bordeaux, where a distance of 110 yards (100 meters) can mean huge shifts in style. But they're also easily identifiable in places like California's Napa Valley, where there are big differences between, say, Stag's Leap and Rutherford, though they're just a few miles apart.

Generally speaking, more and more wineries are realizing that to get real complexity in their Cabernet Sauvignon, they need to plant it in a place that allows the grape to ripen fully, but isn't too hot. The slower the ripening, the longer the time to let flavors build up in the grape, so it's not just full of sugar, but character as well.

There's another change in fashion that's started to emerge over the last few years: namely, blending Cabernet Sauvignon with other grapes. This has always been the case in Bordeaux, where Cabernet's tougher tannins and good color blend well with the fleshier (and flashier) Merlot.

The New World countries, though, went another route. When they imported the grape, they left the French way of thinking behind and made 100% Cabernet Sauvignons (also known as "single varietal" wines). But now we're starting to see a gradual return to the Bordeaux style, frequently using the very same grape varieties that are grown in Cabernet's French heartland.

Like most things in wine, these preferences are cyclical. It may be a modern industry, yet in some respects it's still as old as the hills.

So a grape is a grape is a grape, right? Wrong. Hundreds of factors affect the flavor of each bottle. Some of these factors are determined by the people in charge of the vineyards and the winery. For instance, when to pick the grapes or how exactly to treat the wine during production.

But much of what determines a wine's taste is out of man's control, dependent as it is on the climate and geography of the region (terroir, remember?), plus of course the vagaries of each year's weather.

This is why wine is so beguiling; the way in which it is simultaneously a perfect snapshot of the year it was made and the philosophy of the people who made it, as well as being a reflection of a place's tradition and heritage. Given so many variables at work, is it any wonder that every country has its own ideas about how to get the most out of Cabernet Sauvignon?

EXPLORING

If you're searching for the spiritual home of Cabernet Sauvignon, there's only one place you need to look.

bordeaux

It was from here that cuttings of the vine first made their way across the seas to places like California, Chile, and Australia. Centuries ago, this is where the Cabernet revolution started. Yet Bordeaux's relationship with the world's favorite red grape is not quite as straightforward as you might think. For a start, Cabernet's only been in the region for 300 or so years—far less than its other big red grape variety, Merlot. Plus there's twice as much of the latter as there is of Cabernet Sauvignon.

Second, just about every Bordeaux red wine is a blend of at least two and sometimes as many as five grape varietals. Australia, California, and the like might produce 100 percent Cabernet Sauvignons and take great pride in labeling them as such, but in Bordeaux, blending has always been king. In many ways this makes perfect sense, since Cabernet and Merlot, particularly, work very well together. While the latter is often associated with round, plummy flavors, Cabernet is darker and more brooding; it gives structure to Merlot's softness.

At least, it does when it's fully ripe. Bordeaux is close to the cutoff point beyond which it's not possible to ripen Cabernet Sauvignon, and in cool years the grape can be on the thin side, with enough tannin to push your gums back into your head.

So why, you might wonder, would anyone bother planting the grape in a place that carries with it a risk of failure? Why not plant somewhere warmer and drier; somewhere more reliable?

The answer is that Bordeaux, along with the occasional year we'd all rather forget, also carries with it the tantalizing possibility of years that hit the heights. Years that give not simply good or fantastic wine, but truly great wine that is still talked about in hushed tones 50 years later.

This is the reason Bordeaux is still seen as the beating heart of the wine world today. It's not the size of the place, though at 250,000 acres (100,000 hectares) of vineyard it has about as much area under vine as Chile. Nor is it the 50 plus "appellations" (sub-regions), which have done their best to baffle all but the most dedicated wine lovers through the ages.

It's because, quite simply, Bordeaux makes more of the world's top wines than anywhere else on the planet.

The legendary châteaux of Bordeaux and their famous old vineyards set the standards to which so many other wineries aspire.

Lafite, Latour, Margaux; Haut-Brion and Mouton-Rothschild; Pétrus and Le Pin; Cheval Blanc and Palmer. We could go on for hours talking about these legendary châteaux and their famous old vineyards, which set the standards to which so many other wineries aspire.

So what exactly is it that makes Bordeaux so special? That gives it the ability to produce these A-list wines? It's back to our old friend terroir again.

Let's start with the weather. While sun-seeking tourists from farther north might find the summers plenty warm enough, by grape-growing standards they're relatively cool. In the summer it's pretty common to encounter cloudy or even wet conditions; the sort of weather that would make front-page news in Australia or Chile elicits little more than a Gallic shrug in Bordeaux. Yet these hot, rather than searing, temperatures are a major element in Bordeaux's greatness, since it takes the grapes longer to ripen—particularly Cabernet grapes, which are the last to be picked.

It doesn't do much for the blood pressure of the growers, who are often left gazing at the late summer sky and willing their grapes to ripen before the weather breaks. But since the longer a grape is on the vine, the more flavors it will develop, it does make for better wine.

CABERNET COUNTRY

Given that there's so much more Merlot in Bordeaux than Cabernet Sauvignon, and given that the latter can be tough to grow well, you might be puzzled by its A-list status. Well, unfurrow that brow. When Cabernet Sauvignon gets it right, it gets it spectacularly right.

Cabernet Sauvignon is fêted because it's the star grape of the so-called Left Bank. This area west of the Gironde River is home to many of Bordeaux's superstar wines; the Mecca of the wine world. And it's just as well it's got wine to keep it going, because it's not much to look at.

The Graves to the south is practically a suburb of the ever-expanding city of Bordeaux now, while the Médoc, northwest of the city, is hardly the stuff of picture postcards either. It's flat, stony, never more than 150 feet (45 meters) above sea level,

and with soil so poor that only vines will grow. No livestock, no agriculture, nada.

And that, in fact, is the secret. The intensely stony soil was dumped here millions of years ago by an obliging glacier, and is both incredibly poor and incredibly free-draining. These two factors force the vines to push their roots deep into the earth in search of nutrition and water. In wine terms, this is a good thing, since the deeper the roots go, the more likely they are to come across interesting minerals to add complexity to the grapes' flavor.

There's also the advantage that the stones littering the land's surface (and there are plenty of them on the Left Bank) store heat during the day and radiate it back up to the grapes. For a varietal like Cabernet, which can need a bit of coaxing to attain full ripeness, this, again, is a good thing.

THE GREAT MÉDOC VILLAGES

In addition to wine classified Médoc, Bordeaux's Cabernet country also has a series of "communes" —regional classifications grouped around villages. These names have passed into wine world folklore.

Heading north by northwest out of Bordeaux, the first commune you reach is Margaux. Its wines are lighter and more elegant than those of their northern neighbors: all finesse and silky perfume.

Head on through the central Médoc and you'll get to St-Julien, which has no "first growths" (see right), but a higher proportion of "cru classé" (classed growth) wines than anywhere else. The wines are a beguiling combination of fruit and delicacy, often with slightly cedary notes.

Next is Pauillac, for many people the holy of holies, with the purest expression of Cabernet in the world. The wines are bigger here than elsewhere on the Médoc: darker in color, deeper, rounder, more blackcurranty. Châteaux Mouton, Lafite and Latour, and many others, make the finest of fine wine.

The most northerly of the famous four communes is St-Estèphe, again with a stack of seriously good classed growth properties. The wines here are powerful and mouth-filling, perhaps lacking some of the perfume of their near neighbors to the south.

So close and yet all so different. The way wine styles change, not just from area to area but from producer to producer, is the story of Bordeaux. It's what makes the place hard to understand, even exasperating. But it's also what makes it so special.

THE FIRST GROWTHS OF THE MÉDOC

There are just five first growth wines in the Médoc. The crème de la crème of the wine world, they are Châteaux Haut-Brion, Lafite, Latour, Margaux, and Mouton-Rothschild. All five major in Cabernet.

The wines owe their status to a classification of 1855, whereby those that fetched the highest prices at auction over a number of years gained first growth or "premier cru" status to confirm their superiority.

There are a further four cru classé levels in the Médoc, from second to fifth growths. These are still very good wines, and fetch pretty serious prices.

rest of france

Since Bordeaux is Cabernet's heartland, and plants don't respect lines on a map, it's no great surprise that the grape should have spread out beyond its borders.

Nearby regions in the Dordogne and southwest also have a fair bit of the stuff planted, of which Bergerac, to the west, is probably the most significant. Bergerac doesn't, it's true, have exactly the same soils or microclimate as Bordeaux, but it's pretty close, and it can still knock out a decent bottle of Cabernet. This is frequently blended with Cabernet Franc to give a freshly fruited, raspberryish wine, and though for the most part the wines are designed for drinking young, some can age—especially from good years. There's more than a little truth in the region's description as "the poor man's Bordeaux."

There is a lesser amount of Cabernet Sauvignon in the beautiful Loire Valley, but planting it there always seems to carry more than a whiff of masochism on the part of the grower. That extra 185 miles (300 km) farther north makes a big difference in terms of getting such a sun-hungry grape ripe, and unless it's an exceptionally hot year (such as 2003), the wines can be tannic, a bit on the slim side, and low in color and alcohol.

No such problems in the deep south, where Cabernet's influence is on the up. Its growing success is linked to the increasing popularity of the "vin de pays" classification, which was established there in 1973. Until then, growers either had to make lowly vin de table (the refuge of the desperate) or, if they wanted to label their wine with the superior "appellation d'origine" classification, they couldn't use Cabernet, because it wasn't a grape typical of the area.

Vin de pays, however, is a more flexible animal altogether, allowing all sorts of non-native grapes, among them Cabernet Sauvignon. And now the world's supermarkets are seeing more and more good, ripe, fruity single varietal Cabernets proudly labeled Vin de Pays d'Oc from the south of France. It's not, for the most part, particularly complex, but it's honest, fairly priced, and highly drinkable.

If you want proof of the south's potential with the grape, Mas de Daumas Gassac, northwest of Montpellier, has shown just what the region can do when it really gets its act together. Using Bordeaux grapes, it is one of the iconic wines not just of the south, but the whole of France.

wineries to watch
rest of france

MAS DE DAUMAS GASSAC (LANGUEDOC)

CHÂTEAU POUCHAUD-LARQUEY (BERGERAC)

DOMAINE DE L'ANCIENNE (BERGERAC)

Supermarkets are seeing good, ripe, fruity single varietal Cabernets proudly labeled Vin de Pays d'Oc.

italy

Think Italy and what comes to mind?
Pride, passion, confusion, and sheer bloody-mindedness.

All these are characteristics that run through Italy's wine world, and they go a long way to explaining how Cabernet Sauvignon fits into the scheme of things there.

Let's start with pride. The Italians have a stack of local grape varieties of their own, giving wines of a particular traditional style, and they're touchy about the thought of changing that. Hence, Cabernet Sauvignon (a French invader) has not exactly been welcomed with open arms. It may be the wine drinker's favorite red grape, but Italy—fittingly, given its shape—has largely given it the boot.

Cabernet does exist in the northeast of the country, up around Bologna, Verona, and Venice, which, as a former trade-route crossroads, has always been better about assimilating foreign ideas. There, the grape is usually blended in small amounts with local varietals, and although the Veneto in particular has a tradition of using it to make single varietal wine, Cabernet in Italy is best known for its role in a group of wines called Supertuscans. Which brings us to passion.

Supertuscans are wines from Tuscany, the area that gave us Chianti. They were created when some highly quality-driven producers became frustrated with the rules and regulations governing production of the region's wine, particularly only being allowed to use the local Sangiovese grape, which they felt was limited on its own.

So they tore up the rule book and planted "outsider" grapes, especially Cabernet Sauvignon. This was then either made as a single varietal wine (such as the famous Sassicaia) or blended with the local Sangiovese grape (such as in Tignanello).

The ensuing wines were, by anyone's standards, fantastic, and before long were selling for huge sums of money. Yet in spite of this, because they contained an outsider grape variety, the wines had to be labeled "vino da tavola" (table wine)—the lowest of the country's wine classifications.

But eventually, as bottle prices of Supertuscans spiraled toward the cost of a small space shuttle, the authorities in Tuscany realized how ridiculous it was that some of the country's best wines were outside the supposed quality system. So they introduced a more flexible IGT classification (a bit like French vin de pays), which would give the Supertuscans a new home and allow them to say where they were from on the label.

In spite of this, some producers today still prefer to plow their own furrow defiantly and insist on the vino da tavola classification. Like I said, pride, passion, confusion, and sheer bloody-mindedness...

wineries to watch
italy

ANTINORI

CAFAGGIO

ISOLE E OLENA

PLANETA

SASSICAIA

spain and portugal

Considering that Spain has more area under vine than any other country and that Cabernet is that most peripatetic of grapes, you'd expect to find stacks of it in Spain. But you won't.

Spanish vineyards may stretch for mile after mile on the country's high plains, but comparatively little of what is planted there is Cabernet Sauvignon. Most is Grenache (which also grows all over the south of France) and Tempranillo, a variety grown only in Spain and, to a far lesser extent, Argentina. It is these two grapes (along with a couple of other, smaller varietals), not the regal Monsieur Cabernet, that account for the great historic wines of Rioja and the wallet-busters of Ribera del Duero.

But look a bit more closely and it's there. For starters, while not widely planted in Ribera del Duero, Cabernet is an integral component in the region's (and arguably the country's) most famous red wine, Vega Sicilia. And even though it's not officially allowed in Rioja, Cabernet is still lurking in the background. It arrived there in the 1860s, when Bordeaux's château owners were temporarily chased out of their corner of France by a louse (phylloxera) that ate the roots of their vines. Some settled in Rioja where, as well as introducing the idea of aging wine in barrels, they also brought Cabernet Sauvignon. Only a couple of the oldest estates are officially allowed to use it, but a few other wineries are grudgingly permitted to grow small amounts for "experimental" purposes.

While it's understandable that the Riojans want to hang on to their culture, this is also something of a shame, because Cabernet and Tempranillo mix extremely well, the Spanish grape playing the softer, rounder role taken by Merlot in Bordeaux, and Cabernet adding its usual color and structure.

If it's single varietal Spanish Cabernet you want, look elsewhere. Rioja's neighbor, Navarra, funnily enough, has quite a bit of it and hasn't been shy about ditching the local grapes to make straight Cab, while some of the regions around Barcelona make great wines with it. Penedès, southwest of the city, has some straight Cabernet, but here, as in Bordeaux, it's often blended. The same goes for Priorato, where it's mixed with ancient vines to give wines of real power and quality.

PORTUGAL

Portugal has no wines containing Cabernet that can compete with those in Spain in terms of quality. This isn't surprising, given that the grape is only now tentatively making its presence felt.

Most of the plantings are in the Alentejo, southeast of Lisbon, which has become a giant open-air testing ground. While there's no reason they can't get it right, most Portuguese are hugely proud of their zillions of weirdly named indigenous varietals, and it's hard to see the newcomer (even one with such an impressive pedigree) ever taking over.

wineries to watch
spain

ALVARO PALACIOS

GUELBENZU

MIGUEL TORRES

VEGA SICILIA

wineries to watch
portugal

ESPORÃO

QUINTA DAS PANCAS

rest of europe and lebanon

BULGARIA

I can't help but feel a bit sorry for Bulgaria. For tens of thousands of people who first discovered wine in the mid-1980s to mid-1990s, it was Bulgaria's half-decent bottles of Cabernet that did the trick. Wine, we found out, could be red and dry, and still be drinkable. And if there was an element of "rough and ready" along with the exuberant blackcurrant fruit, that didn't matter because it was so ridiculously affordable.

Bulgaria is the country that everyone forgets they used to drink. It did all the hard work, being cheap, reasonably reliable, and accessible, only for we fickle souls to swan off with more glamorous surf-bunnies from Down Under in the 1990s.

Yet when it comes to Cabernet Sauvignon, Bulgaria is still a major player that is reckoned, even today, to have more of the grape planted than California. There, though, the similarity ends. Whereas Cabernet vines in the Napa Valley are cosseted like toy poodles to produce terrifyingly expensive bottles, their Bulgarian counterparts are driven hard to knock out gazillions of bottles for the world's supermarkets.

It doesn't mean that the wines are necessarily bad, but it is true that the country is having a hard time moving on from where it was 20 years ago. In this, its past isn't helping. Dismantling the communist wine cooperative system and sorting out the nightmarish tangle of who owns the vineyards has certainly slowed the wineries' progress over the last decade. But when it's all done and dusted, don't be surprised to see Bulgaria's huge Cabernet industry rise from the ashes once more.

After all, it has plenty of old, well-established vineyards, a great climate with hot days tempered by cool nights, and more and more investment from outsiders who can see the country's potential and are prepared to put money into realizing it. Some day soon we might even find someone who produces a bottle of really, really good stuff.

winery to watch

bulgaria

BLUERIDGE

HUNGARY AND GREECE

If Bulgaria is a sleeping giant when it comes to Cabernet Sauvignon, these two are more like sleeping minnows. Both have a long and proud wine tradition, and long lists of largely unpronounceable local grape varieties to which they remain fiercely committed. They are slowly starting to use Cabernet to good effect—indeed, it is now the most widely planted non-native varietal in both Hungary and Greece. But it remains very much a minority interest.

LEBANON

Lebanon, do I hear you cry? Yes, Lebanon. The country's French links account for Cabernet's presence in the Levant, and it is widely used by three of the best known producers there: Château Musar, Château Kefraya, and Château Ksara, who have built good reputations on the back of it.

How, you may wonder, can a grape that works in the temperate climate of Bordeaux also work in the Middle East? The answer is the hillsides of the Bekaa Valley. Growing grapes at 1,000 feet (300 meters) above sea level helps them to cool off at night.

Even so, you need a fair bit of dedication. Serge Hochar at Château Musar used to dodge shellfire as he took his precious grapes to the winery during the civil war. No wonder the wine has become a cult classic.

wineries to watch
lebanon

CHÂTEAU KEFRAYA

CHÂTEAU KSARA

CHÂTEAU MUSAR

The USA is one of the biggest wine-producing countries in the world—
and the vast majority of it comes from California.

california

The Golden State has more than a thousand wineries, scattered over a vineyard area that runs about 620 miles (1,000 km) north to south. And while the Chileans and, particularly, the Australians might just have something to say about it, California sees itself, with some justification, as Cabernet Sauvignon's New World spiritual home.

American wine drinkers love the stuff, and the state's producers have gone long on it in recent years. Thousands of acres of the grape have been planted, with hundreds of thousands of dollars invested in wineries to make top-notch wine.

It wasn't always the picture of gleaming success you'll see today, though. The industry has had to wrestle with having its vineyards decimated by phylloxera (the vine-root-eating louse that attacked Bordeaux, remember) and Prohibition in the 1920s, which saw many wineries go bust.

For much of the 20th century, this was an industry in decline, and when Robert Mondavi opened his winery in Napa in 1966, it was the first new one for 40 years. The skeptical locals called it "Bob's Folly." Nonetheless, it was a seminal moment for Californian wine, and heralded a major change in attitude. Rather than knocking out gallons of glug from the hot, flat, and irrigated Central Valley, Mondavi, and the people who followed him, set their sights high. They were trying to create great wine like the best European châteaux did.

And right at the heart of their philosophy were two things: the Napa Valley and Cabernet Sauvignon. Napa is to California what Bordeaux is to France: a brand name recognizable the world over. And like its French counterpart, it has discovered an amazing affinity with Cabernet.

California sees itself, with some justification, as Cabernet's New World spiritual home.

It is this grape more than any other that put Napa (and California wine in general) on the map. With more sun and more reliable weather than in its French heartland, California winemakers can ripen Cabernet more easily, and have developed a style to fit their climate. In a word, the style can be characterized by "ripeness." If in doubt, growers leave their fruit on the vine to make sure tannins are super-ripe and the "mouthfeel" is soft and generous, with no hint of toughness or astringency. Some claret purists may sniff at this approachable style of wine, but the fact that it is accessible younger doesn't appear to be hampering the ability of the top bottles to age for many years—nor their ability to command astronomical prices.

Napa Valley itself is not big. It's only 30 miles (48 km) from top to bottom, no more than five miles (eight km) across at its widest point, and makes just 5 percent of California's wine. Yet within its boundaries are huge changes in style influenced by two main factors: temperature and soil. The soils are richer on the valley floor, giving wines of more power and rather less finesse than up on the valley sides. There are rumored to be more different soil types in the Valley than there are in the whole of France, and while this is a subject that generally concerns American viticulturists less than their French counterparts, some areas are definitely special, of which more in a second.

Although growers have tended to bypass the ground under their feet, there's no way they could ignore the big swings in temperature. The southern end of the Valley, where it opens out into the San Francisco Bay, is way cooler than the north. The south is about as cool-climate as you can get for grapes, while 30 miles (48 km) north, away from the cooling influence of the Pacific, it's too hot for many varieties. In between, though, is a little slice of Cabernet heaven. The best area is reckoned to be

around Oakville and Rutherford, about halfway up. In addition to being the perfect temperature, it also benefits from a particular soil type affectionately known as "Rutherford Dust," which gives these wines an extra minerally complexity.

To the southeast, the cooler Stag's Leap district tends to make wines with a bit less power and rather more elegant perfume—slightly more blackberry than blackcurrant. Elsewhere in Napa, as the "easy" land has become planted, so incomers have had to plant in more remote, often higher and cooler locations. Some of these new wines are stunning, but they are also, because of their cooler sites, frequently tougher, tighter, and (whisper it) a bit more Bordelais in style.

Cabernet's California HQ might be in Napa, but there's plenty elsewhere. The hot, arid Central Valley has seen enormous plantings of it in recent years—most aimed at the cheaper end of the market. Sonoma, to the west of Napa, grows more grapes than its neighbor, but it's cooler and, therefore, much of it is less well suited to Cabernet. However, Sonoma has so many variations of slope, altitude, and fog impact from the sea that it's no surprise to find several areas doing great things with the grape.

Knights Valley is essentially the northern extension of Napa, so we should perhaps expect to find good Cabernet there, but its neighboring Alexander Valley is probably the pick of the bunch. Sheltered from the Pacific's influence by a convenient range of hills, its super-ripe, chocolatey wines are making real waves.

Napa Valley is not big. Yet within it are huge changes in style influenced by temperature and soil.

Waves, in fact, are what stopped Cabernet's progress south of San Francisco. You might think as you move farther south that it would get hotter and, therefore, easier to ripen the grape. Well, it's true, there is more sun and heat. But big gaps in the coastal mountain ranges also mean plenty of cool winds and fogs, which ooze in off the Pacific and drop the temperature dramatically. This is bad news for Cabernet. Most attempts at the grape down here were so unripe they tasted of canned asparagus and acquired the unflattering but accurate nickname of "Monterey Veggies."

There are a few exceptions, though; places sheltered from the breeze and away from the fog. Ridge, high up in the hills around Santa Cruz, is one of the country's best wineries, with a fine Cabernet-dominated wine. But generally speaking, for decent Cabernet, you need to head past the salad bowl of Salinas and Steinbeck country to Paso Robles.

The vineyards here are sheltered from the Pacific by 3,300 foot- (1,000 m-) high hills, so it stays hot (and fog free) all day, but, with no sea influence, the temperature drops dramatically at night. The result: good ripeness, but without those jammy flavors associated with too much heat.

Many wineries set up operations down here in the 1990s as costs in Napa spiraled, and their faith seems (no pun intended) to be bearing fruit. Robles Cabernets are typically soft, ripe, and juicy, with good fruit and less marked tannin. Since they haven't been around that long, the jury is out on whether they will age well, but they certainly deliver plenty of bang for your buck, as a string of top awards in international wine competitions proves.

Outside California, the most promising American Cabernets come from the high, dry, arid vineyards of Washington State to the north.

CULT WINES — AMERICA'S FIRST GROWTHS

America is home to so-called cult wines. These are super-concentrated wines (usually Cabernets) from small estates, typically made in tiny quantities and selling for astronomical prices. Some liken them to their French equivalents in Bordeaux.

Though the wines themselves are of a very high standard, ordering them in a restaurant or buying them at auction has became for many collectors less about the wine itself than about the status it conveys. It is a badge to show off their wealth rather than any real guarantee of wine quality.

In 2000, a six-liter bottle of Screaming Eagle sold for $500,000. This might be exceptional, but bids north of $500 for a 75cl bottle are the norm.

Famous "cult" wines include Screaming Eagle, Harlan Estate, and Bryant Family Vineyard. B-list wines include Opus One, Ridge, and Diamond Creek.

wineries to watch
california

CLOS DU BOIS

CLOS DU VAL

EBERLE

FRANCISCAN ESTATE

ROBERT MONDAVI

SHAFER

STAG'S LEAP

Over the last decade, Chilean Cabernet Sauvignon has become one of the world's most popular tipples. Well-priced, soft, and with stacks of cheerful fruit flavors, it's not hard to see why.

Though the sight of Cabernet from west of the Andes is a fairly recent one for most wine drinkers, don't make the mistake of thinking that this is a young industry, or that Cabernet is a new arrival. The first vines of any description arrived in Chile with Spanish missionaries in the 1500s, while the first French grape varieties made their way into the country in the mid- to late 19th century. Among them was the star of the Médoc, Cabernet Sauvignon. It was often accompanied by French winemakers, who were out of work following the trashing of their own vineyards by phylloxera and had come to seek employment in the new oh-so-chic wine estates being set up by nouveau riche businessmen.

chile

Having decent vines overseen by experienced professionals gave Cabernet a head start in Chile, and the country's climate did the rest in cementing its success. Chile has been described as "God's own vineyard," and that really isn't quite as hyperbolic as it sounds, particularly if your idea of good wine is attractive reliability rather than erratic genius.

Winters here give the vines enough rain to keep them happy, while summers are long, sun-filled, and consistent. Wineries are allowed to irrigate (mostly with melt water from the Andes), and hail isn't a problem as it is for the neighbors in Argentina.

Since it rarely rains between October and April, when the vines are growing and grapes ripening, being a grower in Chile is about as stressfree as it gets. And for a grape like Cabernet, which needs plenty of sun and also ripens later than most, you could hardly ask for more. No wonder plantings of the grape have quadrupled in the last ten years to make it Chile's biggest varietal by some distance.

Nearly all Chile's vines grow in the Central Valley—a long, thin strip of green sandwiched between the Andes and the much lower coastal range of mountains near the Pacific. Aconcagua Valley is the only major wine-producing region north of the capital, with the rest—Maipo, Rapel, Maule, and Bío-Bío—extending 375 miles (600 km) south.

wineries to watch
chile

CASA LAPOSTOLLE

CONCHA Y TORO

COUSIÑO MACUL

ERRÁZURIZ

MONTES

Most of the early vines were planted in the Maipo Valley, just south of Santiago, where many of the wealthy businessmen built their estates. Half a day's horse ride from the capital, it also has the advantage, as you approach the Andes, of well-drained alluvial soils of the sort Cabernet simply loves. Remember the gravels of the Médoc?

Then, of course, there's the small matter of the Andes just off to the east, which, as you might expect, given that they're 23,000 feet (7,000 meters) high, have a not insignificant effect on the local climate. Vines bask in the sun all day, soaking up the heat, while cool air tumbling down off the towering mountains in the evening helps stop the flavors from getting jammy.

The result is Cabernets that are full-bodied but elegant, and sometimes with a little brushing of eucalyptus. Some of the country's most expensive Cabernet Sauvignons, like Almaviva and Viñedo Chadwick, come from Puente Alto in Maipo.

With so much Cabernet planted in the country, obviously not all of it is in five-star sites like Puente Alto, but Chile's great strength is its ability to turn out good, honest, reliable (some might say boring) Cabernets even from unexciting vineyard sites.

Having said all that, the country is on a constant search for more top-class areas. The Colchagua Valley in Rapel, just to the south, is generally better known for Cabernet's big buddy, Merlot. But away from the Merlot-friendly clay soils of the valley floor, winemakers have discovered a real opportunity for Cabernet. The horseshoe-shaped valley of Apalta is producing some wonderful expressions of the grape in a style that is richer, softer, and more chocolatey than those from Maipo.

And the Chileans are nowhere near finished exploring yet. Their string bean of a country has dozens of nooks and crannies that will be suitable for top class cultivation of their favorite grape. Watch this space.

argentina and mexico

There are only 80 miles (130 km) between Chile's Central Valley and Argentina's vinous heartland of Mendoza.

In a plane, you can hop it in just over half an hour. By road ... well, that's another story. The two areas are separated by the dizzying peaks of the Andes, by differing histories, and by different attitudes. Geographically close they may be, but they might almost as well be continents apart.

Where Chile, for instance, has long had a history of successfully growing Cabernet Sauvignon, Argentina has come to the grape comparatively late, and only partly through choice. As the enormous home wine market collapsed in the late 1980s, the wineries needed to make wines that could be sold abroad. And that meant Cabernet Sauvignon.

Climatically, Chile and Argentina are very different, too. Where Chile has the cooling influence of the Pacific, Mendoza has to rely on altitude to stop the vines from frying in the relentless sun. As a result, her vineyards are some of the highest in the world, located from 2,000 feet (600 meters) to an astonishing 4,600 feet (1,400 meters) above sea level.

Then there's the climate. As you might expect, given that they're on opposite sides of a 23,000 foot- (7,000 meter-) mountain range, those of Argentina and Chile are pretty different. In fact, while the latter's is enviably consistent, Argentina's climate can be decidedly tricky. Oh, sure, there's plenty of sun. In fact, Mendoza would be a desert without the irrigating influence of man. But what little rain there is falls not in the winter (which would be helpful), but in the growing season. Worse still, it often falls as hail, which can wreck a vineyard in minutes. Being a grower in Mendoza is not a job for those of a nervous disposition.

Malbec, rather than Cabernet, is Argentina's most popular red grape—and makes far more approachable wine than it does in its homeland in Cahors, in the southwest of France. But Cabernet is on the up as well, and we're starting to see more of it hit the shelves.

The Argentinians usually blend Cabernet with Malbec in a way that would give the good folk of Cahors a heart attack, but they are also increasingly selling it as single varietal wine.

The Cabernets from higher altitude areas of Argentina are lighter and brighter, whereas those from lower levels where it's decidedly hot are big, rich, and positively crying out for a giant, macho Argentine fillet steak!

MEXICO

Yes, that's right: Mexico. It's not all tequila, you know—in fact, there's a pretty big wine industry there. Most of it is dedicated to producing the sort of wines your mother warned you about, but there are a few modernizers, such as L.A. Cetto, Monte Xanic, and Santo Tomás, who have planted European grapes and are doing their best to make modern wine. And some of it isn't half bad either.

The best Cabernets come from up in the Guadalupe Valley, just a giant stride from the southern California border and benefiting from the same cooling influence of the Pacific. The Cabernet here is frequently blended with other grape varieties, such as Shiraz or Merlot.

wineries to watch
argentina

CATENA

FINCA FLICHMAN

ZUCCARDI

wineries to watch
mexico

L.A. CETTO

MONTE XANIC

SANTO TOMÁS

You'll find Cabernet Sauvignon just about everywhere
that grapes are grown Down Under.

australia

From the dark, brooding powerhouse wines of Mudgee a few hundred miles west of Sydney to the new plantings down on the country's temperate southwest coast and the optimists in cool, windy Tasmania, Aussie Cab comes in a big variety of styles—certainly more than a blinkered claret-o-phile would ever want to admit to.

Cabernet isn't Australia's biggest red varietal—inky, peppery Shiraz holds that honor—but it's seen a huge increase in plantings over the last decade, and for many wineries interested in making a top-end wine, Cabernet remains the grape of choice.

Although it's been in Australia since the 1840s, the grape has only really appeared in numbers since the 1970s, and it's taken the industry a while to figure out where it grows best. Huge areas are still given over to Cabernet in the hot, dry, irrigated expanses of the Aussie interior, which are responsible for 60 percent of the country's production. In places like the Riverina, hours of burning sun bring Cabernet to ripeness year after year and give wines with decent color, alcohol, and flavor—but no real character. You can't help feeling that a regal grape like this deserves better, which is perhaps why ever more wineries are moving their Cabernet plantings to cooler sites near the coast.

Cooler in Australia, of course, is relative. And the country has the big advantage that even in the sites nearer the ocean or up on hillsides, there's still plenty of sun to get the grape up to full ripeness and avoid any danger of green or weedy flavors.

Coonawarra is a good example. It's quite a long way south of Australia's wine center of Adelaide; and, not far from the sea, it's pretty cool—in fact, wet and miserable—for much of the year. But it has a warm, dry summer that is perfect for getting Cabernet to peak ripeness. It also has "terra rossa" soil.

Coonawarra's terra rossa is as famous to Cabernet lovers as the gravels of the Médoc or Napa's Rutherford Dust. It's a strip of almost luminous reddy-orange soil about 10 miles (15 km) long by a maximum of 1¼ miles (2 km) wide, and to Australian growers it signals prime Cabernet terroir.

Why? Well, first off it's slightly raised from the surrounding countryside, which is more Irish bog than Aussie desert. Next, it drains easily. Third, the terra rossa sits on a bench of limestone, which means that the vines are able to fossick for nutrients. And finally it's 13 feet (4 meters) above a reliably pure water table (important in Australia), easily reachable by determined vines.

The Coonawarra Cabernets (it even sounds poetic!) are powerful cassis-flavored wines with big, ripe tannins and brooding leather, earth, and licorice elements, which age superbly. By common consent, they're the best that South Australia has to offer, though there are other good areas, too. McLaren Vale, just south of Adelaide, is hotter and gives similarly black-fruited wines (often with a brush of chocolate), and those of the Barossa Valley are big, bold, and heady.

Head east into Victoria and it's a different story altogether. This used to be the beating heart of Australia's wine world and, following a spectacular collapse around the turn of the last century, is now back with a bang. The Yarra Valley, just east of Melbourne, is distinctly cool, even in its warmer areas. It's not often that you'll find good sparkling wines made where Cabernet is grown, but they do it here. The Cabernets are lighter and more delicate in style—the Margaux to Coonawarra's Pauillac—with berry, leaf, and mint aromas.

Coonawarra, Victoria, and the Barossa were all planted in the 19th century, but for many the best

area for Cabernet in Australia is one of the most recent. Margaret River, 125 miles (200 km) south of Perth on the country's western coast, has a more moderate climate than its (very) distant neighbors. The first serious plantings began in the 1960s, when doctors decided that it offered climatic similarities to Bordeaux without the dangers of spring frost.

Well, they got that right—though they reckoned without the strong winds that could batter a vine senseless when it was trying to "set" its fruit, or the kangaroos that chomped the young shoots. For all that, though, Margaret River's Cabernets (often "Bordeaux blends" with Merlot, Cabernet Franc, and so on) are winning admirers the world over for their elegance and finesse. The sandy and gravely soils drain well, the temperatures are less fierce than those in South Australia, and the wines are typified by a mulberry blackberry leafiness and a pretty full tannic finish, rather like those in Bordeaux.

Unlike Bordeaux, though, Australia is always changing. The inquisitive Aussies— using a combination of technology and instinct —are always looking for new sites. It's one of the reasons that the Cabernet story here is about as exciting as anywhere on the planet.

wineries to watch

australia

	CAPE MENTELLE	KATNOOK	TORBRECK
BOWEN ESTATE	COLDSTREAM HILLS	PENFOLDS	WOLF BLASS
BRL HARDY	CULLEN	PETALUMA	YALUMBA

new zealand

The fact that New Zealand's two most popular grape varieties are white, Sauvignon Blanc and Chardonnay, and that Cabernet Sauvignon has gone from third to fifth in the popularity stakes over the last five years should tell you something.

Namely, that most of New Zealand is not terribly well suited to growing it. The South Island is simply too cold, which is why it's a good home to those cooler climate-loving grapes Sauvignon Blanc (Cabernet's mom, remember?) and Pinot Noir, while much of the warmer North Island is simply too fertile and too damp.

When you get vines on fertile soils, they look fantastically healthy, sprouting out shoots and lush leaves all over the place. But that's no good to a winemaker, who

wants that energy to go into ripening fruit, not growing greenery. This is particularly true of Cabernet, which maybe more than any other grape varietal really needs ripeness if it is to give good wine.

The Kiwis, being resourceful folks, and as stubborn as the sheep that litter their countryside, have refused to be beaten, however. For starters, they've brought in different clones of Cabernet, which ripen better in their less exuberantly sunny climate. Plus, they've played around with different ways of trimming the vine, so that it focuses its energy on ripening fruit, rather than growing leaves. They've also, after a few false starts, concentrated their efforts on growing the grape in places that can ripen it properly, which means Waiheke Island near Auckland (boutique wineries, expensive bottles), a few producers east of Wellington, and especially Hawke's Bay.

Two-thirds of the way down the North Island, Hawke's Bay centers around the Art Deco town of Napier. This is New Zealand's driest area, where the sun ricochets off the whitewashed and pastel-colored buildings day after day. In a decent year, it's plenty warm enough here to get Cabernet ripe, though cooler vintages can be a bit tough.

Hawke's Bay's best area is a free-draining former river bed called the Gimblett Gravels. The 34 lucky wineries with land on "the gravels" have even grouped together to form an association bounded by their "unique gravely terroir," a sentence that could have been lifted straight from a pamphlet of Médoc producers.

And while New Zealand's Cabernets are still New World rather than European in style, they're less so than those of their Australian neighbors. In a good vintage you'll find Cabernet's darker fruits leavened with something lighter and more aromatic, while still having delightfully wispy tannins. Not bad with New Zealand lamb, in fact.

wineries to watch
new zealand

| CJ PASK | MONTANA | TE MATA |
| ESK VALLEY | STONYRIDGE | VILLA MARIA |

Visit the vineyards of South Africa and you'll find yourself
wondering just how such an ugly political system could ever
have existed in such a magnificent place.

south africa

Chile may have a more reliably perfect climate, Bordeaux more famous names, and California's offerings attract higher prices, but nowhere in the Cabernet atlas can beat South Africa when it comes to jaw-dropping scenery. No doubt about it, the wine country of the Cape is home to some of the most beautiful vineyards in the world.

Beautiful, yes, but scratch below the surface and, until recently, you'd have found a far less pretty picture. To start with, much of the vineyard area was planted with substandard white grapes that were used either for churning out oceans of unremarkable bargain white wine or for making brandy. The heat of the southern African summer might have led you to expect vineyards full of red grapes ripening in the sun; but a look among the vines would have told a different story.

Not only that, but most of the vines themselves were diseased and struggled to get grapes ripe. Growers couldn't buy more because of economic sanctions, so simply left grapes on the vine for ages to try to ripen them. The result was the worst of both worlds: unripe mouth-puckering tannins and overripe stewed-fruit flavors, which winemakers misguidedly tried to pass off as "the local style."

Fortunately, the last decade has seen huge changes. A more open-minded attitude, combined with the lifting of sanctions, has led to huge amounts of replanting, both to get rid of tuckered-out old vines and to replace those uninspiring white "brandy grapes" with something more user-friendly.

One of the main beneficiaries of all this has been Cabernet Sauvignon, which has grown to become South Africa's most significant red grape. And if you're talking Cabernet in South Africa, you're likely to be talking about Stellenbosch.

Some in South Africa have likened the area to Napa, and while it's far bigger than its California cousin, there are a few similarities. One of these is its position half an hour's drive from a trendy, tourist-friendly city (Cape Town to Napa's San Francisco); another is its growing association with the grape of Bordeaux's Left Bank.

The Cabernet Sauvignon grape hasn't taken over in Stellenbosch to anything like the extent that it has in Napa, and there's been so much experimental planting of different varieties in South Africa over the last ten years that it's going to take a while to figure out whether it ever will. But, for all that, Stellenbosch contains more Cabernet than anywhere else in the country.

One of the benefits of Stellenbosch is that it manages to combine plenty of sun (to help get tough old Cabernet ripe) with significant cooling influences, which help to preserve finesse and prevent the wines from becoming stodgy. These can either be the 1,300 foot- (400 meter-) high vineyards of places like the Simonsberg or the winds that rip in off both the Atlantic (southwesterly) and the Indian Ocean to the southeast.

Either way, they affect the flavor of the wines. Farther inland, in the oven of Paarl, for instance, Cabernets can take on a super-rich, almost meaty character, while Stellenbosch offers brighter, more cultured fruit characteristics.

Frankly, though, it's not easy to generalize too much about Cape Cabernets yet— mainly because the wineries are, to a large extent, still finding their feet with the grape: working out where grows it best and how to get the most out of it. While the locals might tell you that they make "Old World wines from the New World," or that their wines are "halfway between Europe and Australia," it's hard to see that as anything much more than an attractive soundbite.

Stylistically, South Africa's Cabernets can vary from elegant and minerally to fabulously ripe and lush, from single varietal wines to a five-way Bordeaux blend, from open and approachable to closed, tannic, and designed for the long haul.

Then of course, there are the Cape Blends. These mix the local Pinotage grape with the classic grapes of Bordeaux—and the country is fiercely divided about them. Some see it as a point of difference in an ever more homogenized world, others think that Pinotage's "otherness" can't make up for its shortcomings as a grape.

If you're talking Cabernet in South Africa, you're likely to be talking about Stellenbosch.

Either way, most wineries, whatever their feelings about Pinotage, have three or four different Cabernets in their portfolio, covering the whole price range from Wednesday Night to Special Occasion, from simple to complex.

Confusing it might be, but it's also exhilarating, and while this is very much a country in the throes of experimentation, there are enough really good Cabernets coming out at all price levels and in all styles to make it obvious that the grape has a big future here.

wineries to watch
south africa

BOEKENHOUTSKLOOF

DE TOREN

DE TRAFFORD

JORDAN

NEIL ELLIS

RUST EN VREDE

RUSTENBERG

THELEMA

VERGELEGEN

WARWICK

WATERFORD

So much for the places that produce the world's Cabernet Sauvignon. But once you've bought a bottle—whether it's from Bordeaux or the Barossa—how are you going to get the most out of it?

After all, the best bottle of wine in the world is going to taste pretty lousy if it's stored in the wrong way, served at the wrong time in a crummy glass, and drunk with the wrong food.

This is the section where the winery's influence stops and you take over. A few minutes spent finding out what—and what not—to do will make a big difference to your enjoyment of King Cabernet.

ENJOYING

Tasting wine properly (as opposed to just glugging it back) is one of those things that people tend to get embarrassed about.

But there's a good reason for all the swirling, sniffing, and spitting: namely, to bring as many of your senses into play in assessing the wine as you can.

As for the spitting, that's only necessary if you're tasting a whole stack of wines; there's no need to do it at the dinner table!

GETTING THE BASICS RIGHT

Don't go overboard, but there are a couple of things here that make a big difference. Number one: Get a decent-sized glass that will allow you to swirl the wine around a lot. Number two: Make sure the wine is at the right temperature.

For reds, this means room temperature, but if your house is like a sauna, you might want to find a slightly cooler room in which to store it. When a wine is too hot, the alcohol is exaggerated; when it's too cold, the flavors are subdued. 61–64°F (16–18°C) is a good temperature.

When a wine is too hot, the alcohol is exaggerated; when it's too cold, the flavors are subdued.

how to taste

WHAT NEXT?

Fill your glass about a third of the way and look at the color. If it's a bright vibrant ruby, that means it's still young. If it's got browner hues at the edge, it's aging. If it's cloudy, it means it's faulty.

NOSE POWER!

Swirl the wine around a bit (now you see why you need a big glass) and take a good sniff. It should smell of fruit, not grapes. Typical for Cabernet are black fruits, such as blackcurrants, black cherries, mulberries, and damsons. Other aromas you might find are mint, eucalyptus, dark chocolate, cedar, tobacco, olives, and cigar boxes. Oh, and cinnamon spice from oak barrels. The main thing is to go with your instincts. If you think a wine smells of old car tires or chocolate cake, then say so!

AND FINALLY...

Take a sip and sloosh it around your mouth. How full-bodied is it? Is it sweet or dry? If it dries your teeth and gums, that's tannin coming into play. But is there too much, or is it in balance? What does it feel like in your mouth? After you've swallowed, for how long afterward can you taste it? Most importantly, did you like it? Remember, tasting is totally subjective; there are no right or wrong answers.

Remember, tasting is subjective: there are no right or wrong answers.

So you've bought
your bottle of Cabernet
Sauvignon. How should
you look after it?

The short answer is that, if you're only
going to hang onto a wine for a couple of
weeks, short of storing it in the oven, it
doesn't much matter. But if you want to
keep your wine for months or years, there
are a few things to get right.

The keys to storing wine are
temperature and light—and wine doesn't
like too much of either. That's why,
historically, it was stored in cellars. Since
few houses have cellars nowadays, you want
to try and find a place that is dark, as cool
as possible, and at a reasonably constant
temperature. About 50–54°F (10–12°C) is
fine, but better to have it a bit too warm,
but dark and constant (under the stairs,
perhaps), than cold for six months and hot
for six months (for example, under the
eaves or in the garage).

storing and when to drink

When to drink a wine is trickier, since it depends on the style of the wine itself and your own preferences. If you drink a top Bordeaux too young, the tannins will strip the enamel from your teeth, because it's designed to be drunk 20 years from vintage. But sit on a cheap bottle of Bulgarian, and the flavors will have died in three years.

The good news is that most wines now—and especially those from the New World—are softer, rounder, and more "fruit-forward" than they used to be. Probably 95 percent of all the Cabernets on the market can be drunk young, no problem at all, and most of them are well made enough to age at least a few years.

What you have to remember is that the longer you leave a wine, the fewer "fruit" aromas you will get, and the more complex "secondary" aromas like leather, spice, tobacco, or even farmyard (!) you will find. How much of one or the other you want is a question of your personal preferences. Just remember that wine stored somewhere warm ages faster than wine stored somewhere cool.

When it comes to actually serving the stuff, the bigger the glass the better. Try to get the wine at the right temperature (see How to Taste, page 56), and decant it beforehand if you can. You don't need a swanky crystal decanter either. Just pour the wine into a pitcher, then back into the bottle. This will get some oxygen into the wine and free up its flavors.

A good way around the "when to drink" dilemma is to buy, say, three bottles (or a case if you're feeling flush) of a wine. That way you can spread the consumption out over a few years and see how a wine develops with time.

matching
cabernet and food

One of the great things about wine is also one of the things that makes it difficult to get a perfect food match: namely, the way in which it changes from country to country, from region to region and from year to year.

Now, our friend Cabernet may be one of the world's more reliable grapes, but it still comes in as many different styles as there are bottles on the planet. Stylistically, there is a world of difference between, say, an everyday bottle of Bordeaux and a $50 bottle of Napa Valley Cabernet. The latter will probably taste sweeter and richer, with big powerful baskets of black fruit bursting out of the glass, and gentle tannins. The cheap Bordeaux, by contrast, will be both lighter in color and taste, and probably with more evident tannins and acidity—especially if it's from a cooler vintage.

The bad news about food and wine matching is that it's almost impossible to be really precise. The good news is that you don't need to be, and a few general guidelines will get you through most situations. Generally speaking, the "bigger" the Cabernet, the more powerful the food will need to be.

Cabernet comes in as many different styles as there are bottles on the planet.

TOP BOTTLES

So, big, rich New World offerings (like our $50 Napa Cab) or top Bordeaux wines are happiest up against great lumps of rare red meat: steak and other beef dishes are classic matches, but heavier game such as venison works pretty well, too.

MIDDLEWEIGHT CABERNETS

Middleweight wines from cooler climate New World countries or more average wines from warm Bordeaux vintages work with middleweight meat like duck, pheasant, or lamb—particularly if the wine's had a few years aging to tone down some of the in-your-face fruit flavors.

LIGHTER CABERNETS

Lighter varieties (like the cheap Bordeaux or Bergerac) work pretty well with simpler, more rustic food, such as meaty pasta sauces and burgers.

MATCHES TO AVOID

Basically, steer clear of light foods like fish, seafood, salad, or lighter meats such as pork, since a wine as flavorful as Cabernet Sauvignon will just stomp all over them. Spicy food can give you problems as well, because the tannin in the wine exaggerates the heat of the dish. Having said all that, if you enjoy cod curry and Cabernet, go for it!

When all is said and done, your taste in food and wine is as personal as your taste in music, clothes, or life partner. If you like it, that's good enough!

picture credits

index

Thanks to my parents for introducing me to wine at an early age, to my lovely wife, Bola, who has borne my vinous ramblings down the years with great good humor, and to my daughter Rebecca who makes it all worthwhile.

acknowledgments